DEADLY SKIES
AIR WAR 1914-1918

WRITTEN BY JOHN MAKER
ILLUSTRATED BY OUTLAND ENTERTAINMENT

D1520678

CANADIAN WAR MUSEUM
MUSÉE CANADIEN DE LA GUERRE

Library and Archives Canada
Cataloguing in Publication

Maker, John, author
Deadly skies: air war, 1914-1918 /
written by John Maker;
illustrated by Outland Entertainment.

(Souvenir catalogue series, ISSN 2291-6385; 15)
Issued also in French under title:
Un ciel meurtrier.
ISBN 978-0-660-03143-9 (paperback)
Cat. no.: NM23-5/15-2016E

1. World War, 1914-1918 – Aerial operations –
    Exhibitions.
2. World War, 1914-1918 – Aerial operations –
    Comic books, strips, etc.
3. Aeronautics, Military – History –
    20th century – Exhibitions.
4. Aeronautics, Military – History –
    20th century – Comic books, strips, etc.
5. Graphic novels.

I.   Canadian War Museum, issuing body.
II. Outland Entertainment, illustrator.
III. Title.
IV. Series: Souvenir catalogue series; 15.

D600.M35 2016
940.4'4
C2016-902911-5

Published by the
Canadian War Museum
1 Vimy Place
Ottawa, ON K1A 0M8
www.warmuseum.ca

Printed and bound in Canada.

This work is a souvenir of the exhibition **Deadly Skies – Air War, 1914–1918**, which was developed by the Canadian War Museum, with the generous support of the J. P. Bickell Foundation and the Audrey S. Hellyer Charitable Foundation.

Souvenir Catalogue series, 15
ISSN 2291-6385

CONTENTS

INTRODUCTION

The First World War saw the first large-scale use of aircraft in warfare. Each side tried to control the skies to ensure victory on the ground.

Six illustrated stories take you through the danger and exhilaration of military flight training, observation, bombing and aerial combat as they depict unique experiences of the first air war.

A GLOBAL WAR IN THE AIR

The First World War in the air was waged around the world. In most places where fighting took place on the ground and at sea, aircraft were also flying and fighting above. Airplanes, Zeppelins and observation balloons brought the war into the sky like never before.

NORTH AMERICA

DOMINION OF CANADA

Southern Ontario

O Ottawa

UNITED STATES OF AMERICA

Washington O

Marjorie Stinson

San Antonio Texas

O

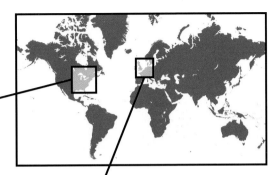

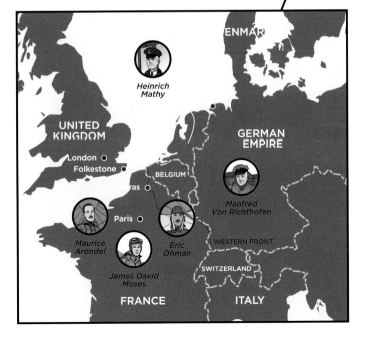

WESTERN EUROPE

TRAINING

In 1914, most aspiring pilots had never set foot in an airplane, and military flight training was informal and improvised. Since there were few flight training programs in Canada, young Canadians trained at one of eleven flying schools in the United States.

In April 1915, the Curtiss Flying School opened in Toronto, but its limited capacity could not meet the growing demand for pilots. In early 1917, the United Kingdom established a program in Canada and in other countries that included classroom lessons and extensive aviation training.

JOIN MARJORIE STINSON,
THE TEENAGED AMERICAN
FLYING INSTRUCTOR, AS SHE
TRAINS YOUNG PILOTS FOR
THE SKIES EARLY IN THE WAR.

15

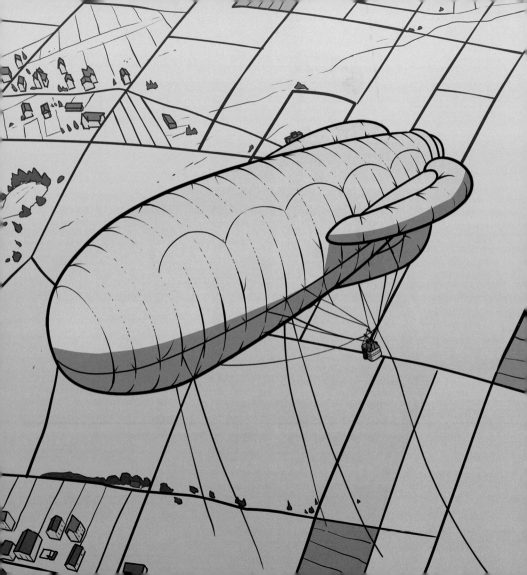

OBSERVATION

Aerial observation, also known as reconnaissance, was the first and most important role of the air forces during the First World War.

As trench warfare emerged in 1914, aircraft became the primary means of gathering information beyond enemy trenches. From observation balloons and reconnaissance airplanes, observers helped direct artillery fire by reporting the fall of artillery shells. They also took photographs of enemy positions. Observers and their pilots had a great impact on the outcome of the war, but lacked the glamour later associated with fighter pilots in aerial duels.

JOIN CANADIAN JAMES MOSES, A WARRIOR OF THE SIX NATIONS CONFEDERACY, AS HE MOVES FROM THE TRENCHES TO THE SKY.

SIX NATIONS OF THE GRAND RIVER
TERRITORY, HAGERSVILLE, ONTARIO
OCTOBER 1916

I'LL BE BACK BEFORE YOU KNOW IT.

I'LL PUT YOU RIGHT HERE, NEXT TO YOUR BROTHER.

KA-BOOM!

26

TAC-A-TAC-A-TAC-A-TAC-A-TAC-TAC

GAS!

THE NEXT MORNING ...

FRANCE, MARCH 30/18
DEAR DAD,
I AM GETTING ALONG O.K. ...

... I AM NOW A FULL-FLEDGED FLYING OFFICER, AND FEEL QUITE PROUD OF IT. FOR IT SURELY MEANS SOMETHING TO GET AN OBSERVER'S WING UP OVER HERE.

... WE ARE INSEPARABLE. QUITE THE WAY PILOT AND OBSERVER SHOULD BE.

... MY PILOT AND I HAVE HAD SOME VERY THRILLING EXPERIENCES JUST LATELY ...

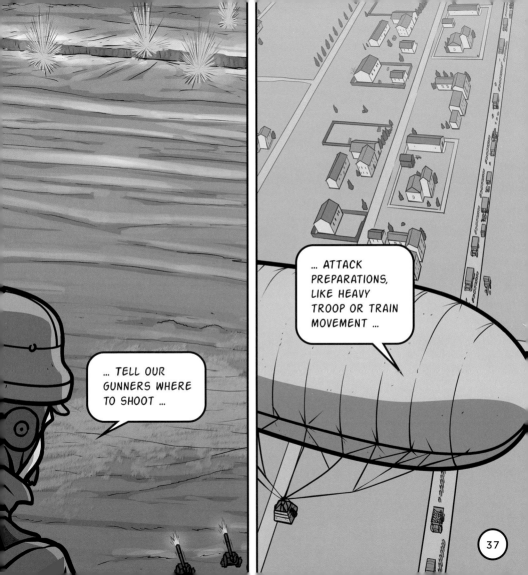

... WHEN ATTACKED, THE MISSION IS PARAMOUNT.

WELL! WEYGAND, I UNDERSTAND. THEY WANT TO DO THAT? WELL! I'LL DO THIS, THIS AND THAT.

EIGHT DAYS LATER ...

LIEUTENANT ARONDEL?

YOU'VE BEEN RECOMMENDED FOR THE LEGION OF HONOUR.

43

BOMBING

The fundamental tactics and strategy of bombing were developed during the First World War. Aerial bombing became much more effective, varied and intense from its introduction in 1914 to the end of the war in 1918.

In 1914, pilots dropped small bombs by hand on targets close to the front lines. By 1917, they carried large bomb loads deep into enemy territory. This enabled both sides to engage in "strategic bombing" against industrial and population centres with airplanes and airships such as Zeppelins. Intended to reduce enemy military and industrial production, strategic bombing brought the war to civilians like never before.

JOIN CAPTAIN HEINRICH
MATHY, A GERMAN ZEPPELIN
COMMANDER, AS HE AND
HIS CREW PREPARE FOR A
BOMBING RAID OVER BRITAIN.

MATHY FAMILY HOME, HAGE, GERMANY
SEPTEMBER 5, 1916

THIS BERLIN NEWSPAPER ARTICLE
(SEPTEMBER 5, 1916) REPORTED
THAT BRITISH DEFENCES HAD
SHOT DOWN A GERMAN ZEPPELIN.

I'M WORRIED, HEINRICH.

DON'T BE, HERTHA. MY CREW IS VERY SKILLED.

ZEPPELIN BASE, NORDHOLZ, GERMANY
SEPTEMBER 6, 1916

THERE WILL BE NO MORE TALK LIKE THAT, PETERS.

... I DREAM CONSTANTLY OF FALLING ZEPPELINS. IT IS AS IF THERE IS A STRANGE, DARK TUNNEL BEFORE ME ...

IT IS ONLY A QUESTION OF TIME BEFORE WE JOIN THE REST. OUR NERVES ARE RUINED ...

YES, CAPTAIN.

MATHY FAMILY HOME
HAGE, GERMANY
OCTOBER 1, 2016

"THE BURIAL OF A GERMAN ZEPPELIN CREW IN LONDON"
BERLINER TAGEBLATT

I HAVE A GIFT FOR YOU. FOR LUCK.

I'LL WEAR IT, AND FEEL YOU NEAR.

52

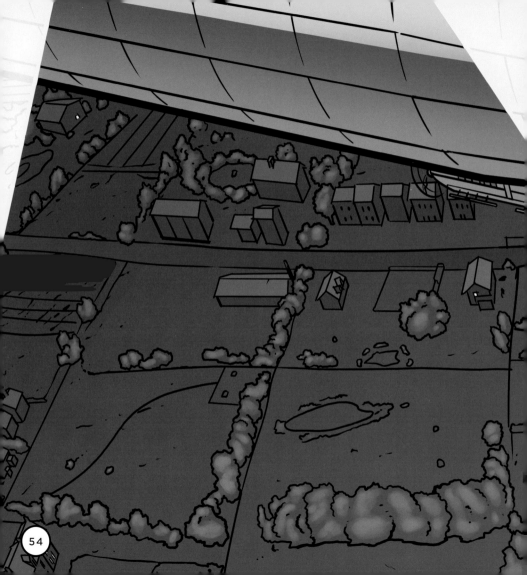

56

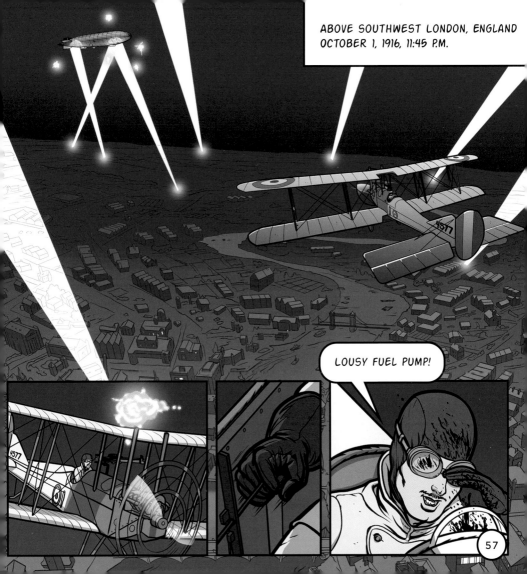

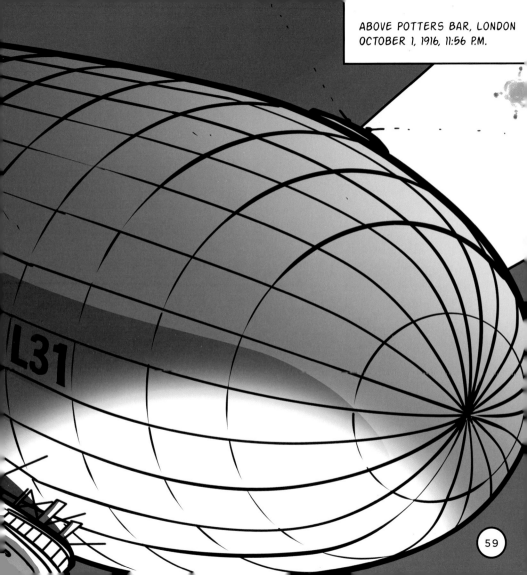

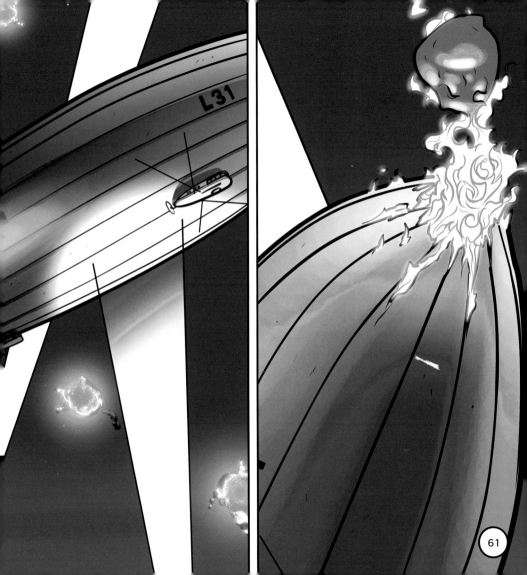

OCTOBER 2, 1916, 12 A.M.

62

AERIAL COMBAT

Aerial combat was initially a means of protecting friendly observation missions and fending off incursions by enemy airplanes. By 1917, however, pilots in groups of fighter airplanes known as squadrons were engaging in major aerial battles for control of the skies.

JOIN MANFRED VON RICHTHOFEN, THE FAMOUS RED BARON, AS HE ENGAGES IN AERIAL COMBAT.

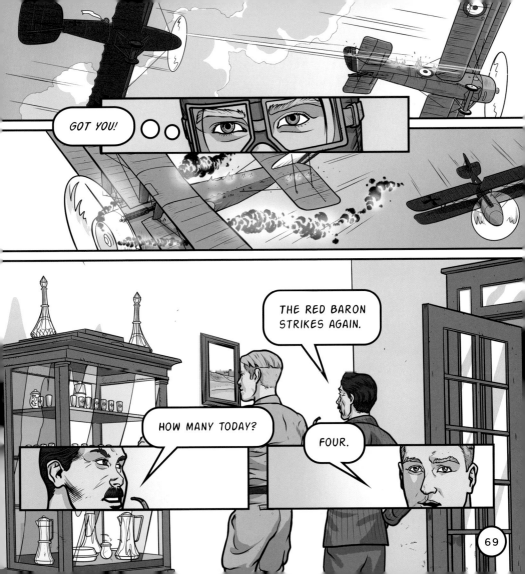

20 DAYS LATER ...

74

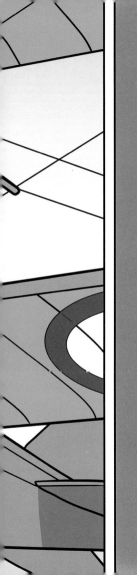

JOIN ERIC OHMAN, A CANADIAN FIGHTER PILOT, AS HE EXPERIENCES THE AIR WAR FIRST-HAND.

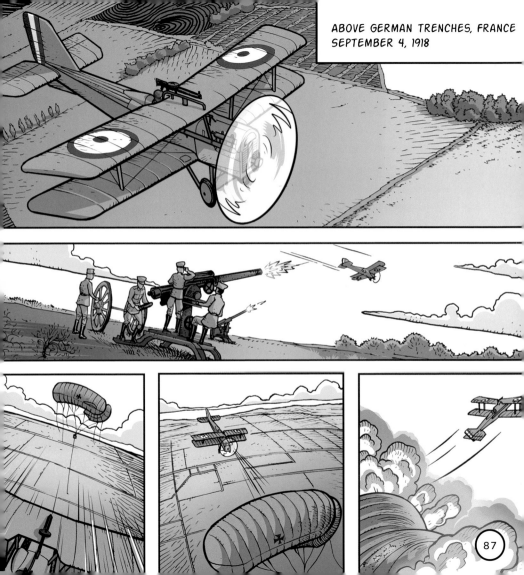

ABOVE GERMAN TRENCHES, FRANCE
SEPTEMBER 4, 1918

87

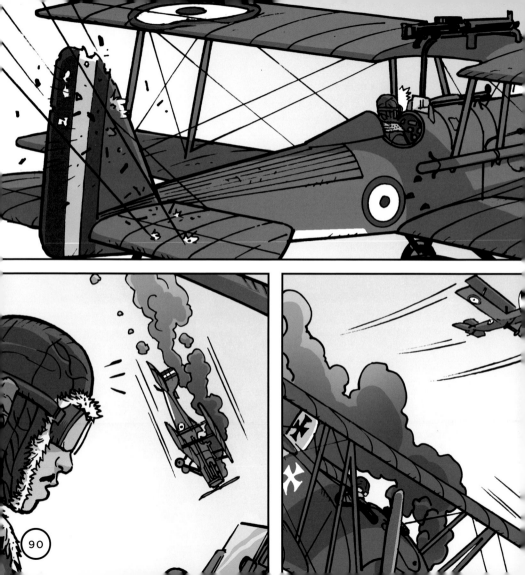

POOR OLD CRAWFORD.

HE DIDN'T LAST LONG.

SO, YOU WANT RED OR BLACK?

THE SQUADRON IS GETTING VERY CALLOUS ABOUT DEATH.

A SOCCER MATCH BETWEEN NO. 10 SQUADRON AND NO. 41 SQUADRON ...

A FEW DAYS LATER, NOON

I'D COUNT MYSELF LUCKY. ONLY THREE OF US CAME BACK FROM FIRST PATROL.

I'M GOING UP THIS AFTERNOON.

HOW'S OUR CASUALTY FEELING TODAY?

ALMOST BETTER, NO THANKS TO THAT BRUTE FROM NO. 10!

GOOD LUCK.

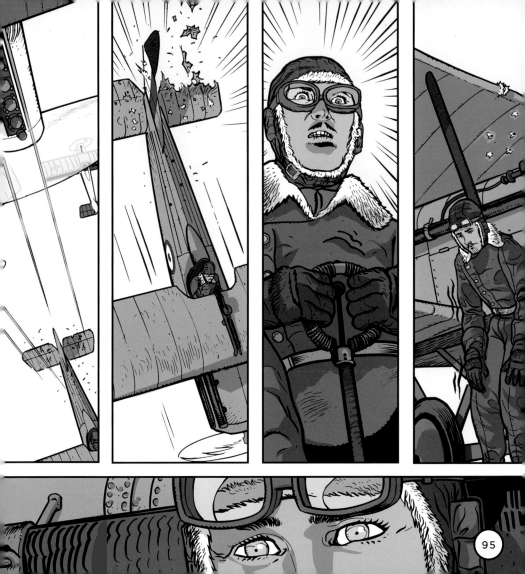

October 7th 1918

Almost the whole original flight has disappeared. First Hemming left, then Turner was wounded, Mitchell missing, Crawford in flames, McGibbin wounded. Morris shot and now prisoner, which leaves me the oldest

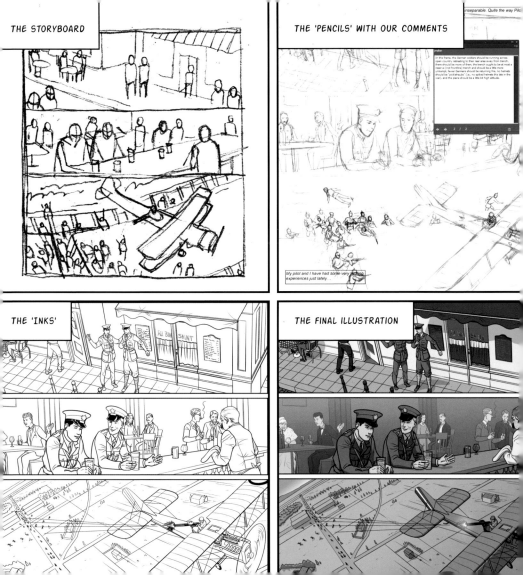

THE STORYBOARD

THE 'PENCILS' WITH OUR COMMENTS

THE 'INKS'

THE FINAL ILLUSTRATION

BEHIND THE SCENES

The six stories you have just seen are all true. By presenting them in vivid colour, the Canadian War Museum team brought the day-to-day realities of the air war to life.

How did we do it? We researched the stories by visiting archives, libraries and museums across Canada, Australia and the United Kingdom, and walking the ground where these events took place.

Working with the illustrators from storyboard to final display, we reviewed drawings, provided feedback, and searched for photographs and colour references to evoke the experiences, people and places depicted.

James Moses's story was derived from his great nephew's recollections and a rich family history. The family provided photographs, poems, newspaper clippings and detailed letters Moses sent home in the days before his death.

Family member John Moses described the interior of the Moses home: "The Moses family of that era aspired to be prosperous farmers by southern Ontario standards, while maintaining Six Nations/United Empire Loyalist roots... there might have been a framed engraving of Joseph Brant on the wall... perhaps surmounted by a small crossed pair of Union Jack flags."

INK DRAWING OF THE MOSES HOME

109

SCRAP OF FABRIC

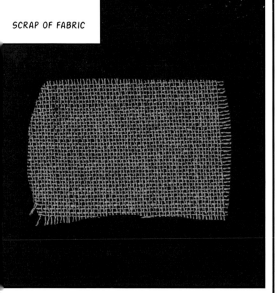

OHMAN'S DRAWING OF HIS LIVING
QUARTERS (REPRODUCTION)

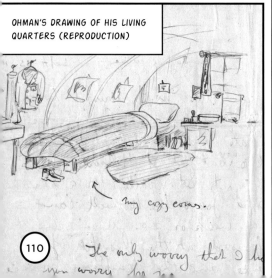

my cozy corner.

The only worry that I h...
you worry ...

Eric Ohman's story was based on a collection of over 500 documents, photographs and artifacts, as well as conversations with his daughter and other family members.

Although a unique personal experience, Ohman's story is also typical of Canadian pilots' experiences of the air war. That is why we felt it was important to tell.

Eric Ohman's family collection includes this piece of fabric from the wall of his quarters at his aerodrome and a drawing he sent to his parents, so that they could see where he was living.

Images courtesy of Audrey Ohman Southward and Gordon Southward

ACKNOWLEDGMENTS

We would like to thank the members of the core exhibition team:
Marie-Louise Deruaz, Nic Clarke, Julie Savard, Britt Braaten, Caroline Dromaguet
and Jessica Shaw. The illustration team: Jeremy Mohler, Lee Oaks, Cesar Diaz,
Andy Poole and Pedro Figue. The design firm Reich+Petch, specifically Edmund Li,
Ron Flood and Helen Lai. We would also like to thank our many colleagues at the
Canadian War Museum and the Canadian Museum of History for providing crucial
assistance and expertise, particularly our colleagues in Collections: Carol Reid,
Maggie Arbour, Susan Ross, Arlene Doucette, Eric Fernberg, Anne Macdonnell,
Meredith MacLean, Lindsay Towle, Mike Miller and Mayme Windle. Thanks also to
historians Andrew Burtch, Mélanie Morin-Pelletier, Peter MacLeod, Joanne Stober,
Krista Cooke, Stacey Barker, Tim Cook, Laura Brandon and Jeff Noakes. Special thanks
are due to Natascha Morrison for her invaluable help in image sourcing. Thanks also
to publications coordinator Lee Wyndham for her excellent work in producing this
souvenir catalogue. We would like to acknowledge the individuals and institutions
whose objects, images and expertise allowed us to produce both the exhibition and
this publication. Finally, we would like to thank the families of the people in this book,
many of whom collaborated to make sure we captured their loved ones' wartime
experiences as accurately as possible.

JAN 2